COOLBEAN
The Soybean

SHAWN CONLEY, Ph.D.
with Judy Mannes & Marsha Rehns

American Society of Agronomy
Crop Science Society of America
Soil Science Society of America
5585 Guilford Road, Madison, WI 53711-5801 USA
608-273-8080
agronomy.org | crops.org | soils.org
dl.sciencesocieties.org | SocietyStore.org

ISBN: 978-0-89118-617-5 (print)
ISBN: 978-0-89118-618-2 (electronic)
doi:10.2136/2013.coolbean
Library of Congress Control Number: 2013956057

ACSESS Publications: ISSN 2165-9834 (print),
ISSN 2165-9842 (online)

Illustrations: John Lambert
Design and production: Kristyn Kalnes

ACKNOWLEDGMENTS:
Palle Pederson for resource photos; Seth Naeve, Bill Wiebold, Chad Lee, Bill Tracy, and Brian Diers for scientific review; Rachel Knoll, Flor Mitchell, and Barb Leach for providing teachers' perspectives and review comments on educational quality. Special thanks to the bright, hard-working students of Midvale Elementary and Gompers Elementary for reviewing a draft of the book.

Printed in the United States of America.

Published with generous support from
The Wisconsin Soybean Marketing Board
A farmer organization focused on improving the Wisconsin soybean industry and its ability to feed the hungry world while being stewards of the land we farm.

Hey there, It's me...Coolbean, the Soybean!
Ready for an adventure? All right, let's roll!
Watch me get planted. Stick around. Soon, I'll change from a **seed** into a plant. A plant that makes...you got it...more soybeans! Nope, it's not magic. That's what cool beans do. Follow me, and you'll find out what else makes soybeans so awesome!

CROPS are plants that people grow for their use. Most crops become food. Others are used to make medicines, fuels, clothes, and other things.

Think like a Scientist...

Scientists use the **scientific method** to study and learn things. They ask questions and use evidence to find answers. Here are the steps they take:

- Ask a question.
- Observe and gather information (research).
- Come up with possible answers (a hypothesis).
- Experiment to test the hypothesis.
- Observe and record the results.
- Decide if the results prove the hypothesis.

Making Better Soybeans

Plant breeders study **traits** of soybean plants, like how many beans they produce. Plants, like people, **inherit** traits from their parents. Plants pass traits to their **offspring** in their seeds.

Plant breeders select seeds from parent plants that have the best example of the trait they are trying to improve. They repeat this process many times until they get plants with the specific trait they want.

OFFSPRING are the descendants of parent plants or animals. Children are the offspring of their parents.

COOL FACTS

Soybeans are **seeds**. When seeds are planted they grow into plants.

In the United States, one farmer feeds about 150 people.

NO-TILL farming is a way of growing crops. Farmers dig up—till—their fields as little as possible. That saves them money and helps to protect the environment.

COOL FACT

When scientists measure things, they use the International System of Units. Temperature is measured in degrees Celsius (°C), and centimeters are used instead of inches.

Now the real action starts. Haila loads my friends and me into containers, called **hoppers,** on the back of a gigantic machine for planting.
Haila, planting is such fun. Why are you so serious today?
I've got a lot on my mind. I need to grow healthy soybeans...and lots of them. Without crops to sell, I can't look after my family.
Wow! I didn't realize you had so many responsibilities.
And that's not all of it. People around the world count on farmers like me for food.
People also depend on me to be a **sustainable farmer**. That means I keep the land, water, and air clean as I grow my crops.
SOYBEANS

COOL FACT

Soybeans are planted on more than 77 million acres of U.S. farmland. That's the same size as the state of New Mexico.

Weed Control

Haila spaces the rows close together, about 15 inches (38 centimeters) apart. As the soybean plants grow, their leaves spread out and shade the soil between the rows. That helps to stop **weeds** from growing.

Do Something Cool...

Each bag of seeds that Haila used contained 140,000 seeds. To calculate how many bags she needed to plant 2,000 acres, go to the activity "Soybean Seed Calculator" at **www.coolbeanthesoybean.org.**

The Right Soil for Soybeans

The best soil for soybeans is loose and crumbly. Small spaces in the soil, called **pores**, let **oxygen** and water move around a plant's roots. Some water stays in the pores and keeps the soil moist but not soggy. Soggy soil can smother a plant's roots.

NUTRIENTS are chemicals that plants and animals need in order for them to grow and be healthy.

Think like a Scientist...

Coolbean says he likes loose, crumbly soil. If you were a scientist, what experiment would you design to find out if Coolbean is right?

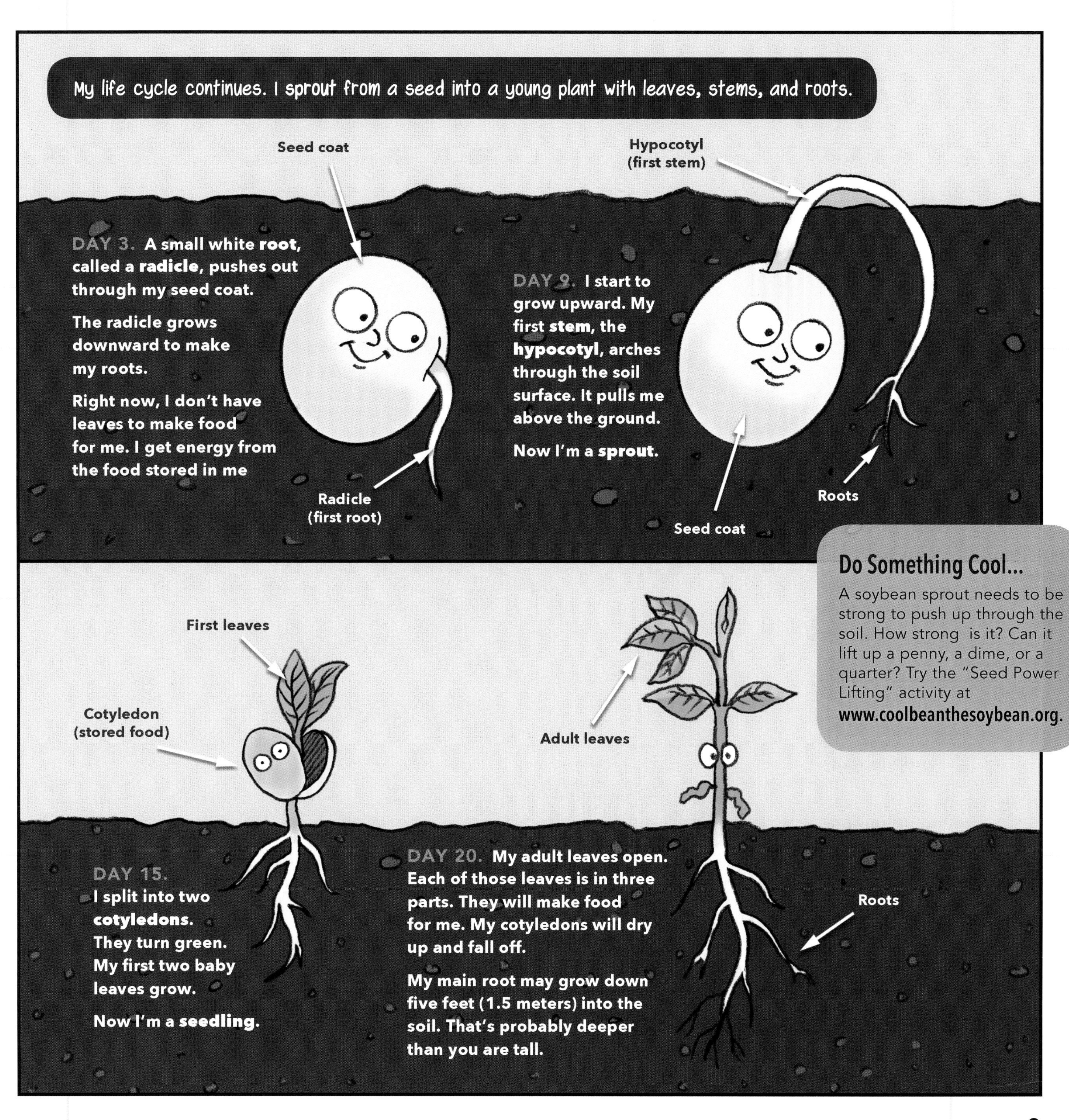

Do Something Cool...

A soybean sprout needs to be strong to push up through the soil. How strong is it? Can it lift up a penny, a dime, or a quarter? Try the "Seed Power Lifting" activity at **www.coolbeanthesoybean.org.**

Crop Rotation

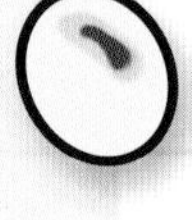

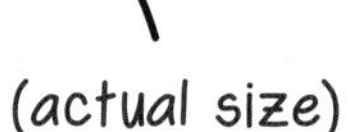

Farmers have been rotating crops for thousands of years.

Alternating the types of crops in the same field produces a larger crop. It also reduces pests.

Famous African American scientist, George Washington Carver, taught southern farmers to rotate cotton with soybeans or peanuts.

We know **crop rotation** is good for plants, but scientists have not unlocked all the secrets of why.

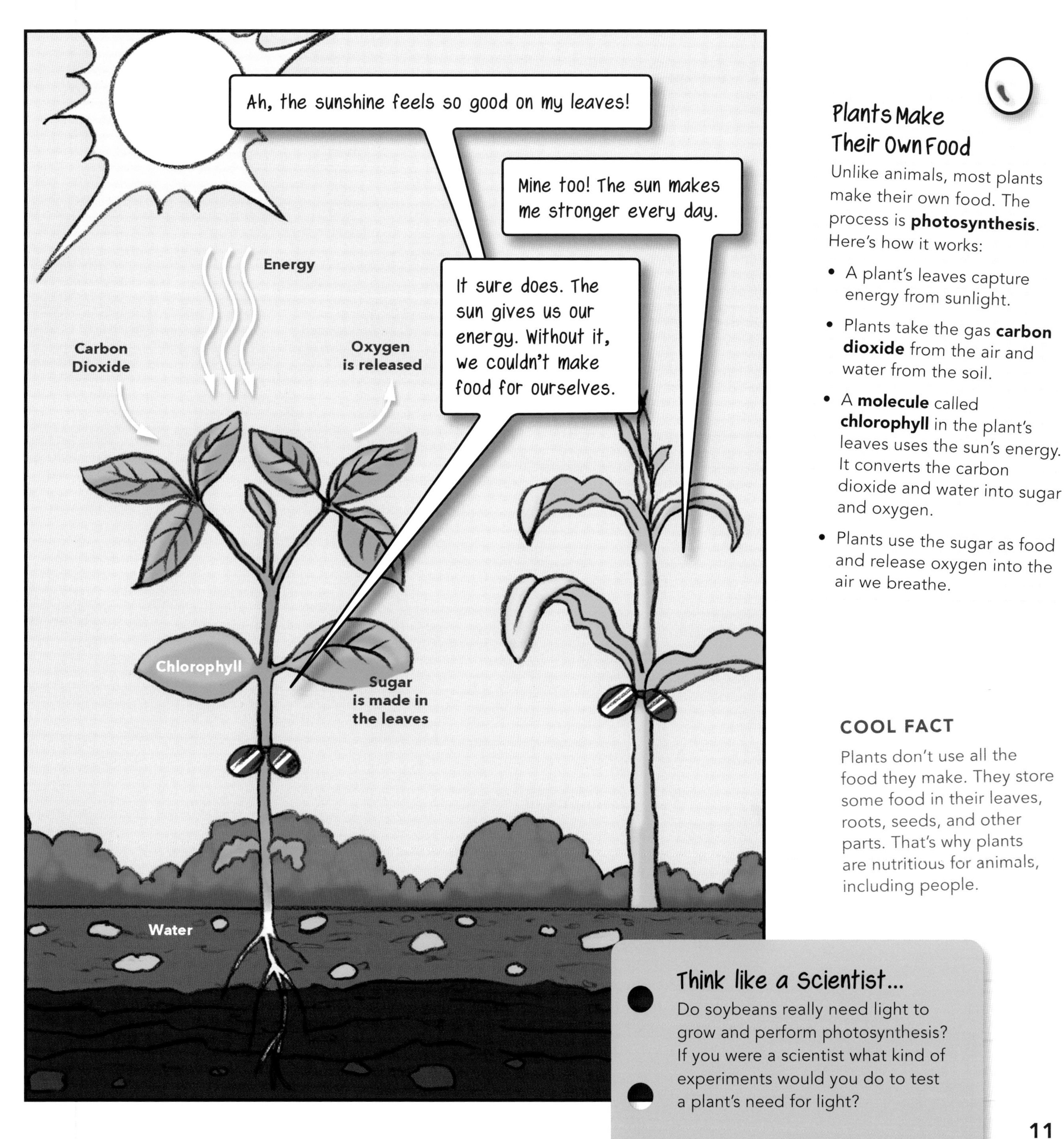

Plants Make Their Own Food

Unlike animals, most plants make their own food. The process is **photosynthesis**. Here's how it works:

- A plant's leaves capture energy from sunlight.
- Plants take the gas **carbon dioxide** from the air and water from the soil.
- A **molecule** called **chlorophyll** in the plant's leaves uses the sun's energy. It converts the carbon dioxide and water into sugar and oxygen.
- Plants use the sugar as food and release oxygen into the air we breathe.

COOL FACT

Plants don't use all the food they make. They store some food in their leaves, roots, seeds, and other parts. That's why plants are nutritious for animals, including people.

Think like a Scientist...

Do soybeans really need light to grow and perform photosynthesis? If you were a scientist what kind of experiments would you do to test a plant's need for light?

NITROGEN is an element essential to all living things.

Nitrogen—It's Essential

Nitrogen is a gas. The air around us is 78 percent nitrogen. But plants can't take nitrogen from the air.

They depend on bacteria to change the nitrogen into a substance they can use.

Soybeans Are Special

Most plants—like corn or wheat—don't have Rhizobia nodules on their roots. But a group of plants called **legumes** have nodules. Soybeans are legumes. Peanuts, peas, and clover are legumes too.

Earthworms Recycle

Earthworms help add nutrients to the soil that plants use as they grow. But earthworms need the help of bacteria. Here's how it works:

- Earthworms eat dead plants in the soil.
- Earthworms have bacteria in their intestines to help them digest the plants.
- Earthworms use some of the digested food as energy. Some of it they excrete (poop) as waste.
- The waste adds nutrients to the soil that growing plants can use.

Now, I know why Earl was so freaked when he saw the bumps on my roots. He must have seen these wanted posters!
I get it. Rhizobia are not the only "bump-makers." There are some really creepy critters out there, like **NEM-A-TODES**!
They are worm-like pests that are seriously gross...and mean! They can chow down on my roots and make me sick.
Sure hope they like those tasty-looking super weeds more than me.
WANTED APHIDS for sucking the Life out of Soybeans!
WANTED CYST NEMATODE Violent Root Attacks!
WANTED The SUPER WEED GANG Wanted for Crimes Against Soybean Society!

AGRONOMISTS are scientists who study and improve soil and plants and help farmers produce more sustainable crops.

Hunting Aphids

In June, Aliah begins to check for aphids in Haila's fields. She uses a magnifying glass to see the aphids. These insects are about 1/16 inch (1.6 mm) long.

Aliah records the number of aphids she finds on each plant. If she finds more than 250 aphids on a plant, she will tell Haila to use insect spray to kill them.

POLLEN is a powder produced by all plants. Plants must have pollen to reproduce.

COOL FACT

Soybeans begin to flower at the end of June as the hours of daylight decrease. They need to make seeds before the summer ends.

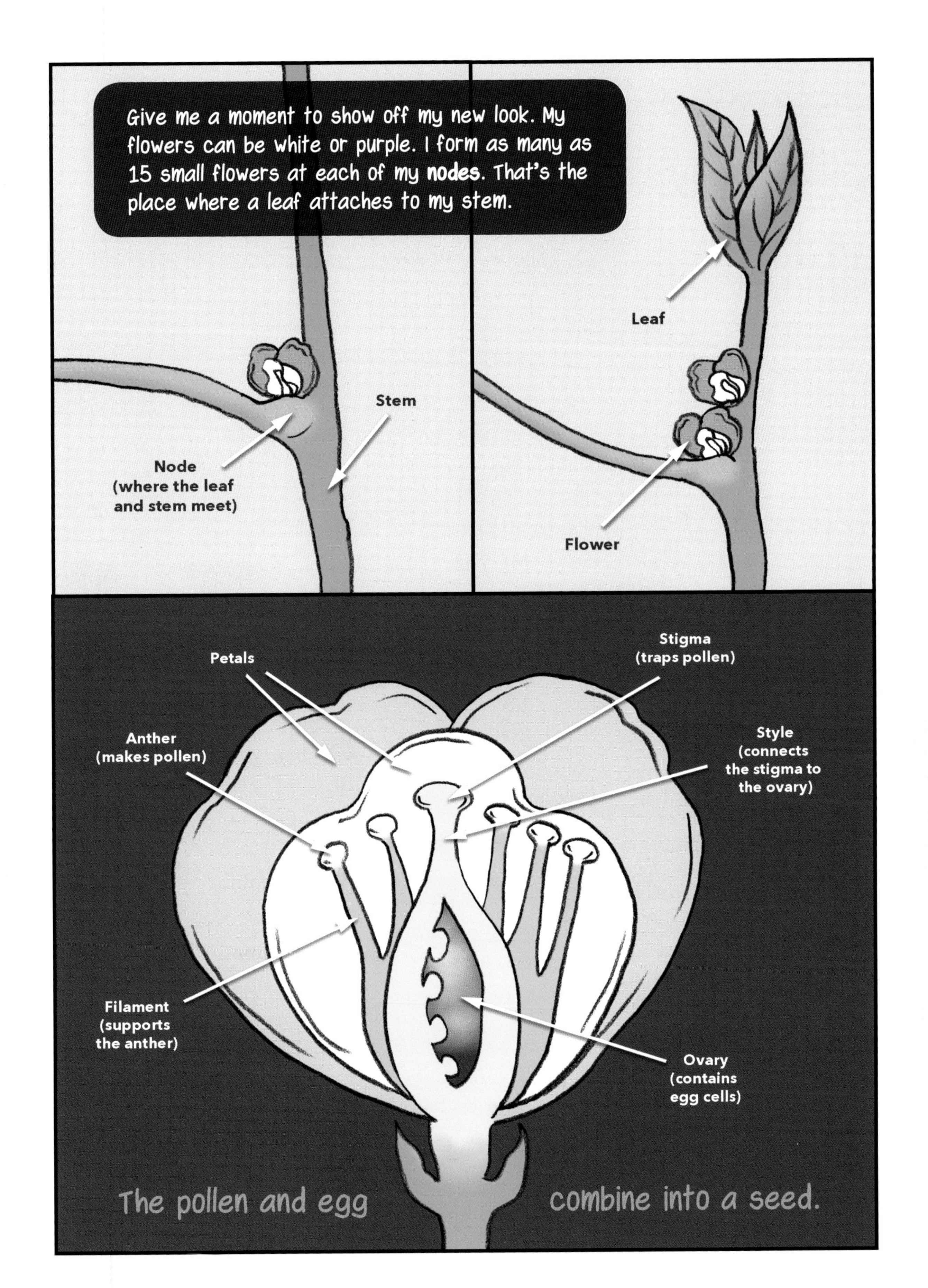

COOL FACT

Only about 1/3 to 1/2 of soybean flowers make pods.

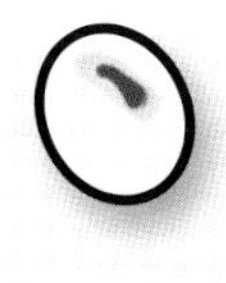

From Flowers to Pods

Soybean flowers have male and female parts. The male parts, called **anthers**, make **pollen**. The sticky grains of pollen fall onto the female part, called the **stigma**, and then travel through the **style** to the **ovary**. This is pollination. It is how a flowering plant reproduces.

The ovary becomes a pod. Each pod will contain one to five seeds, or beans.

Ready for Harvest

Soybean plants turn brown when they are full grown, or mature. The food made by green leaves is now stored in the seeds.

Think like a Scientist...

What would happen if Coolbean got too much or not enough water? If you were a scientist, how would you determine the right amount of water so your soybeans are healthy and you have a good harvest?

Power Food

Some soybeans are harvested when they are still green. Green soybeans are often called edamame.

Most soybeans are harvested when they dry out and turn yellow. They are used in food for animals and people.

Green or yellow, soybeans are loaded with **protein**. One-half cup of cooked soybeans has three times as much protein as one hotdog and much less fat.

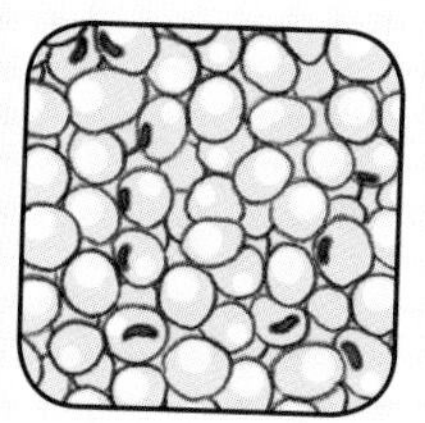

COOL FACT

All animals need protein in their diet. Protein builds muscles, helps to heal wounds, and fights infection. Meat, eggs, dairy products, nuts, and beans all have protein in them.

Do Something Cool...

Roasted soybeans, like peanuts and almonds, can be ground and made into a buttery spread. To make your own, try the "Soynut Butter Recipe" at **www.coolbeanthesoybean.org.**

GOOD LUCK COOL BEAN
Congratulations on another great harvest!
Aliah, we couldn't have done it without your soybean smarts. It's been a lot of work since we planted in May. But wow, it's been worth it.
Soybeans are a great crop. It's really rewarding to grow them because there are so many uses for these super beans.
Aw, thanks! None of us would be here without partners like Haila to grow us.
And after a great growing season, now I have so many choices of where I can go and what I can become.
It's so exciting!
CANDLE

Here Today, Here Tomorrow

Soybeans are a **renewable resource**. They produce seeds that can be planted to make another crop.

Non-renewable resources are things like coal, oil, and gasoline. When they are gone, we can't get any more.

COOL FACT

Henry Ford, who founded the Ford Motor Company, produced an automobile with plastic parts made from soybeans. It weighed less than a metal car so it used less fuel.

Do Something Cool...

How many products with soy in them can you find in your home or grocery store? To find out what to look for on a label, go to the "Soy Scavenger Hunt" activity at **www.coolbeanthesoybean.org.**

COOL FACT

The first soybean seeds planted in America came from China. In 1765, Benjamin Franklin imported them and sent them to a friend to plant in his garden.

Super cool news! I'm going to a farm in China. I want to go where my soybean ancestors came from more than 5,000 years ago. The first soybean farmers were Chinese.
SOYBEANS
SOYBEANS
SOYBEANS
SOYBEANS
SOYBEANS
Life is cool being Coolbean, the Soybean!!

Cool Words

AGRONOMIST: a scientist who studies and improves soil and plants and helps farmers produce more sustainable crops

ANTHER: the male part of a flower that makes pollen

APHID: insect that can damage plants by sucking on their leaves and stems

BREEDING: producing new forms of plants and animals in order to improve them

CARBON DIOXIDE: a gas in the air that plants need to make food

CHLOROPHYLL: the green chemical in plants that makes photosynthesis possible

COMBINE: a machine that cuts and collects (harvests) crop seeds

COTYLEDONS: a plant's first leaves that are the remains of the seed

CROP: plants that people grow for their use. Most crops become food. Others are used to make medicines, fuels, clothes, and other things.

CROP ROTATION: growing different plants in a field from year to year

DATA: pieces of information used to help answer questions

FIELD: an area of ground in which crops are grown

FILAMENT: a male part of a flower that supports the anther

FLOWER: the part of some plants that produces seeds

GERMINATE: to start to grow, the first growth of a seed

GREENHOUSE: a structure, often made of glass or plastic, that keeps the light and temperature the same while plants are growing

HARVEST: gathering a crop

HOPPER: container for seed on a planting machine (planter)

HYPOCOTYL: a plant's first stem

INHERIT: to get traits from a parent

LEGUMES: plants that have bacteria on their roots that provide the plants with nitrogen. Peas and soybeans are legumes.

LIFE CYCLE: different stages of growth a plant or animal passes through

MOLECULE: a small particle composed of two or more atoms

NEMATODE: a tiny worm-like pest that feeds on plant roots

NITROGEN: the most common gas in the air, a building block needed by all living things

NODE: place where a leaf attaches to a stem

NODULE: small swelling on the roots of soybeans and other legumes that contains helpful bacteria

NON-RENEWABLE RESOURCES: products that can't be replaced, such as coal from the ground

NO-TILL FARMING: a way of growing crops. Farmers dig up—till—their fields as little as possible. That saves them money and helps to protect the environment.

NUTRIENTS: chemicals that plants and animals need in order for them to grow and be healthy

OFFSPRING: a descendant of parent plants or animals. Children are the offspring of their parents.

OVARY: a female part of a flower that produces seeds

OXYGEN: a gas in the air that plants and animals need to survive and that you breathe in with every breath

PHOTOSYNTHESIS: the way plants make oxygen and their own food using carbon dioxide, water, and the energy from sunlight

POLLEN: powder-like substance that all plants produce in order to reproduce (make more plants)

PORES: small spaces in the soil that let air and water move around a plant's roots

PROTEIN: one of the three components of food that help make muscle, skin, and blood. (The other two are fat and carbohydrates.)

RADICLE: a plant's first root

RENEWABLE RESOURCES: materials that can be made or collected over and over again, such as crops

REPRODUCE: to make more plants and animals

RHIZOBIA: a family of bacteria that help plants fix (make) their own nitrogen

ROOT: the part of a plant that anchors it to the ground and absorbs water and nutrients from the soil

SCIENTIFIC METHOD: the way scientists study and learn about the world. The scientific method consists of asking a question, gathering information (data) through observation and research, proposing a hypothesis (a possible answer to the question), testing the hypothesis with experiments, recording results of the experiments, analyzing the results, and reaching an answer to the question based on the evidence.

SEED: the part of a plant that can grow into another plant. Many fruits and vegetables, such as carrots, watermelon, and soybeans, grow from seed.

SEEDLING: a young plant

SOIL: a mixture of minerals, organic material, air, and water. Most plants need soil to grow in.

SPROUT: a new plant that has just poked up above the soil

STEM: the part of a plant that grows above ground and holds leaves and flowers

STYLE: a female part of a flower that connects the stigma to the ovary

SUSTAINABLE FARMER: a farmer who grows crops in a way that protects the land, air, and water

TRAIT: characteristic of an individual plant or animal, such as the color of a flower or the shape of a leaf. Traits can be inherited by the individual's offspring.

WEED: an undesirable plant that can rob a crop of water, nutrients, and space to grow in

Dr. Shawn P. Conley is the State Soybean Specialist at the University of Wisconsin–Madison. Shawn in an agronomist! He grew up on a dairy farm and loved playing outdoors with all the animals. Shawn's passion is growing better beans! He is blessed with an incredible wife Lori, two wonderful daughters (Haila and Aliah), and a great dog named Sadie.
After graduating high school I went to school for another 10 years to get my Ph.D. and become a professor. It was hard work, but it was worth it.
A typical day for me is just what you read in the book. I design experiments and conduct research. I scout and take care of soybeans like Aliah. I go to farms like Haila's and help solve problems. I then communicate everything I learn via my webpage, blog, and Twitter. I have the best job in the world.
Cool beans!!!
Shawn's a cool guy. I love scientists!